Baby Animals from Africa

Barb Asselin

Asselin Group Online Publisher
R.R. #2, 449 Flat Rapids Road
Arnprior, ON Canada K7S 3G8

www.AsselinGroup.com

Bonus Activity Book

Thank you for purchasing this book for your child.

As a thank you, I'd love to offer you this fun, free activity
book to
complement our "Baby Animals from Africa" book:

"African Animals Activity Book"
(For more fun with your child ☺)

Download your copy at:

https://asselingroup.leadpages.net/african-animals/

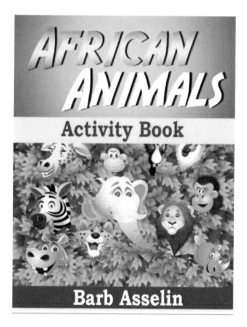

Also by Barb Asselin

About the Author

Barb Asselin is a college professor and best-selling author who has published books in many different genres including education, cooking, law, real estate, internet marketing, entrepreneurship, baby sign language, fitness, office administration, children's fiction and children's non-fiction.

Barb loves writing for children and wrote her first children's book when her first child was just 6 months old. Since then, she has written many children's fiction and non-fiction pieces and her work has been published online and in Appleseeds Magazine.

Since she began teaching in 2004, Barb has taught in six different programs within the School of Business and has created numerous online courses for Algonquin College including the Virtual Assistant program.

She loves to teach through her courses, books, and textbooks, and strives to make a connection with each student and reader. Barb lives in Canada with her husband, Mike, and two adorable daughters, Casey and Jamie. They enjoy music, skiing, golfing, running, and mixed martial arts.

Baby Animals from Africa

Baby Animals from Africa

Hippopotamus

My name is hippopotamus.

My nose is big and round.

I love the mud.

I play in it from sun up til sundown.

My ears are small.

My skin is gray.

I weigh five thousand pounds,

And when I play in mud all day,

I turn from gray to brown.

Lion

The lion is the jungle king.

He prowls and growls and roars.

He sleeps for twenty hours

out of every twenty-four.

Just when you think he's waking up

to prowl and growl some more,

He blinks his very sleepy eyes

and then he starts to snore.

Elephant

Elephants are the biggest animals around.

Africa and Asia are where they can be found.

Their ears are huge and help cool them down.

Their feet are flat and actually quite round.

Elephants' trunks are like another arm, you see.

They are used to pick leaves from the branches of trees

"We love our veggies", the elephants say.

They eat one thousand pounds a day.

Cheetah

The cheetah is a type of cat

with lots and lots of spots.

She has so very many

you could play connect-the-dots.

Her legs have so much power,

She runs sixty miles an hour.

She can outrun anyone

and never get caught.

Giraffe

I'm a giraffe and I'm so tall,

my head is in the trees.

This makes it very easy for me

to munch away on leaves.

I'm so tall a man can only

reach up to my knees,

And all day long I'm on my feet,

even when I catch some ZZZs.

Zebra

The Horse-Tiger is my favorite name,

I'm striped like a tiger with a horse's mane.

My pattern of stripes is unique you see,

It separates every other zebra from me.

My stripes are alternating black and white,

And on my tummy, there's not a stripe in sight.

Africa

The continent of Africa has animals galore,

The hippopotamus, the zebra, the cheetah, and more.

Animals in the north, south, east, and west,

Tell me, which one do you like the best?

Don't Forget Your Free Activity Book

Just visit the link below to download your complimentary African Animals Activity Book – more fun for you and your child!

https://asselingroup.leadpages.net/african-animals/

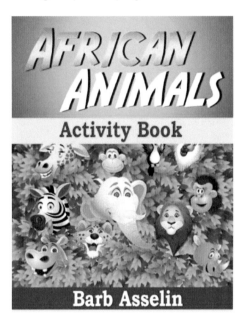

Here is a sneak peek from our children's picture book,
"If I Were in the Circus"...

The circus is coming. It's that time of year.

Shout it out loud, for everyone to hear!

Any day now, the tent will go up.

I'm bringing my friend and she's bringing her pup.

Friends will arrive from here and from there.

They'll come here from just about everywhere.

"I want to go," the cat says today.

"The juggler is my favorite," his friends hear him say.

The balls go up and the balls go down.

The juggler throws them around and around.

I practice with yarn. They work just fine.

If I were in the circus, those balls would be mine!

Enjoy this book?

I see you've made it all the way to the end of my book. I'm so glad you enjoyed it enough to get all the way through! If you liked the book, would you be open to leaving me a 4 or 5 star review? You see, I'm a self-published author, and when people like you are able to give me reviews, it helps me out in a big way. You can leave a review for me at the following link:

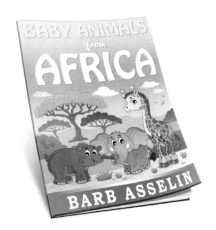

It'd really mean a lot to me.

Thank you.
Barb Asselin

Made in the USA
Monee, IL
06 January 2021